797,885 Books
are available to read at

Forgotten Books

www.ForgottenBooks.com

Forgotten Books' App
Available for mobile, tablet & eReader

ISBN 978-1-331-45264-5
PIBN 10192112

This book is a reproduction of an important historical work. Forgotten Books uses state-of-the-art technology to digitally reconstruct the work, preserving the original format whilst repairing imperfections present in the aged copy. In rare cases, an imperfection in the original, such as a blemish or missing page, may be replicated in our edition. We do, however, repair the vast majority of imperfections successfully; any imperfections that remain are intentionally left to preserve the state of such historical works.

Forgotten Books is a registered trademark of FB &c Ltd.
Copyright © 2017 FB &c Ltd.
FB &c Ltd, Dalton House, 60 Windsor Avenue, London, SW19 2RR.
Company number 08720141. Registered in England and Wales.

For support please visit www.forgottenbooks.com

1 MONTH OF FREE READING

at

www.ForgottenBooks.com

By purchasing this book you are eligible for one month membership to ForgottenBooks.com, giving you unlimited access to our entire collection of over 700,000 titles via our web site and mobile apps.

To claim your free month visit:
www.forgottenbooks.com/free192112

* Offer is valid for 45 days from date of purchase. Terms and conditions apply.

English
Français
Deutsche
Italiano
Español
Português

www.forgottenbooks.com

Mythology Photography **Fiction**
Fishing Christianity **Art** Cooking
Essays Buddhism Freemasonry
Medicine **Biology** Music **Ancient Egypt** Evolution Carpentry Physics
Dance Geology **Mathematics** Fitness
Shakespeare **Folklore** Yoga Marketing
Confidence Immortality Biographies
Poetry **Psychology** Witchcraft
Electronics Chemistry History **Law**
Accounting **Philosophy** Anthropology
Alchemy Drama Quantum Mechanics
Atheism Sexual Health **Ancient History**
Entrepreneurship Languages Sport
Paleontology Needlework Islam
Metaphysics Investment Archaeology
Parenting Statistics Criminology
Motivational

A Nation's Discipline; or, Trials not Judgment

E 458
.1
.D25
Copy 1

A

DISCOURSE

DELIVERED ON THE

NATIONAL FAST DAY, SEPTEMBER 26, 1861

IN

Spring Street Church,

NEW YORK,

BY REV. ROBERT DAVIDSON, D.D

PASTOR.

PUBLISHED BY REQUEST.

NEW YORK:

A Nation's Discipline; or, Trials not Judgments.

A

DISCOURSE

DELIVERED ON THE

NATIONAL FAST DAY, SEPTEMBER 26, 1861,

IN

Spring Street Church,

NEW YORK,

BY REV. ROBERT DAVIDSON, D. D.,

PASTOR.

PUBLISHED BY REQUEST.

NEW YORK:
W. S. DORR, BOOK AND JOB PRINTER, 101 NASSAU STREET.
1861

E 458
.1
D25

DISCOURSE.

"SHOW MY PEOPLE THEIR TRANSGRESSION."—*Isaiah lviii.* 1.

IN accordance with the proclamation of the President of the United States, first recommended by both Houses of Congress, and since concurred in by the Governor of the State, and the Mayor of the City, we have met to observe this day as a day of fasting, humiliation and prayer. We are to observe the day with religious solemnity, sorrowful remembrance of our faults as a nation and as individuals, and the offering of fervent supplications to Almighty God for the safety and welfare of these States, for His blessing on our arms, and for the re-establishment of law, order and peace.

Fasting is a natural concomitant and expression of mourning. The heart heavy with grief "forgets to take bread." Hence fasting is always conjoined in Scripture with penitential sorrow, whether that sorrow be spontaneous or divinely commanded. The outward signs are of value only as the exponent or heightener of the discomfort within. "By the sadness of the countenance the heart is made better;" hence the prophet calls such a day "a day for a man to afflict his soul." By a law of our nature, to put on the weeds of mourning and to enter the sombre apartments of grief predisposes us to sadness; as on the contrary, to assume a gay attire and frequent the company of the cheerful tends to enliven our spirits. But there should be, along with the decorous assumption of the external signs of sorrow, a sincere spirit of penitence and amendment, reformation and charity. "Is not this the fast that I have chosen?" continues the prophet, "to loose the bands of wickedness, to undo the heavy burdens?" Not that God disowns the act of fasting. He only expresses His preference. It is to be interpreted like that passage, "I will have mercy, and not sacrifice," meaning, "rather than sacrifice;" or that other verse, "Thou desirest not sacrifice, else would I give it." God desires not the symbol without the soul; He wishes not the fasting without the repentance and reform. Sacrifices were a divine ordinance, and doubtless David conscientiously offered them.

In the chapter just quoted from Isaiah, the 58th, the prophet rebuked further, the disposition to "fast for strife and debate, and to smite with the fist of wickedness." It is a perversion of the objects of such a day to preach political sermons, to heap reproach on adversaries, and to direct acrimonious invective against political parties whose views do not agree with our own. Such a disputatious temper is not in harmony with the humble and subdued feelings which we should cherish at such a season.

But while such perversions are to be discountenanced, it is a time for speaking the truth. And if political subjects are necessarily brought under review or adverted to in connection with the day, such introduction is not to be confounded with political sermons. A discourse in favor of loyalty, or in reproof of national errors, even though it should involve a glimpse at political questions, can hardly be called political preaching. On the present occasion it is difficult to draw the line between politics and morals. A clergyman is not to abstain from proclaiming that "rebellion is as the sin of witchcraft," because some of his hearers, with secession proclivities, might object to it as political preaching.

The President, the Governor, and the Mayor, have all united in exhorting us to confess and deplore our national sins and transgressions, our faults and crimes, both as a nation and as individuals. Now if we are to humble ourselves and confess our sins, we must know what they are, and distinctly specify them. "Show my people their transgression, and the house of Jacob their sins." We are not to do this in a vague and general and superficial way, but with clearness and minuteness.

What, then, are our NATIONAL SINS ? Some point out Sabbath-breaking, or profanity, or licentiousness, or intemperance, or covetousness, or venality, or slavery. Some omit the latter from their catalogue altogether, or speak of it under their breath, and add cautiously that little should be said about it. I infer this from the published notices of a variety of discourses, (in themselves excellent,) delivered on the last National Fast Day. Some orators enumerated everything that could be with propriety brought in, except only the very point which, in my estimation, was the pith and marrow, the real *gravamen*, of the whole matter. I do not deny that the first mentioned sins have been and are too prevalent. But I do not know that they are more so than formerly; perhaps they are less. At the close of the Revolutionary War, infidel principles, brought over by the French officers, had leavened the people extensively. Paine was not afraid to publish his Age of Reason, and Infidelity, in the person of Thomas Jefferson, was elevated to the seat of the Chief Magistrate. The defeated candidate, Aaron Burr, was equally an unbeliever, and notoriously one of the most immoral of men. Yet for half a century we have gone on prosperously as a nation, and flattering ourselves that we have basked under the peculiar smile of Heaven. Our national anniversaries have rung with self-gratulations and thrasonical vaunts. We have thought our country the envy and admiration of the world, the asylum for the downtrodden and oppressed of every clime. And it must be confessed that there was some shadow of reason for it, when we beheld immigrants from foreign parts flocking to our shores annually by hundreds of thousands, hoping to find in this land of promise a refuge everywhere else refused them. These things are undeniable.

Are we worse now? are we worse than other nations that have no civil or foreign wars? Are we less pious or moral, than the average of other lands? Our Presidents, for a series of years back, have been patterns of morality. Some have been pious men. Some have declined receiving visits on the Lord's day. All have been exemplary in attendance upon divine worship on the Sabbath. As a church-going community, the American people compare favorably with any other, though we rely only on the voluntary principle. Within the last four years there has been an unusual degree of prayer in all parts of the land. Daily prayer meetings were started in countless places; and it was said, perhaps not altogether hyperbolically, that a traveller might go over the length and breadth of the land, and in every place where he would stop he might find a prayer meeting to attend. The Fulton Street prayer meeting, which has attained a world-wide celebrity, has just celebrated (Monday, September 23d,) its fourth anniversary, and there was as crowded an audience as ever, and unflagging interest. Within the interval alluded to, revivals of religion have abounded, and numbers have been brought into the churches, approaching, it is thought, two hundred thousand. The Sabbath Committee has labored indefatigably and successfully to restore the Sabbath to its pristine honors, and grog-shops, and theatres, and music halls, have been compelled to close their doors on that day. (And here it may be remarked in passing, that violations of the Sabbath in the army *since* the war began cannot be adduced fairly as a *cause* of the war before it began.) Some Sunday papers have been of late discontinued, and some Sunday trains have ceased to run. Chaplains accompany our regiments, and prayer meetings are held in the camps. Our soldiers have written home, not for provisions, not for tea and coffee, not for rifles and havelocks, but for hymn books. The daily press has for a considerable time devoted a portion of its columns to religious intelligence and ecclesiastical records, which it would not do without readers. For the second time a National Fast Day is observed; and this time the President has been requested to proclaim it by a Committee of both Houses of Congress.

If all this be true, and he must be hardy who will venture to deny it, then I must own myself at a loss to discover any special provocations of Sabbath breaking, profanity, or other wickedness to draw down unwonted judgments at this particular time. One is tempted to think that there has been of late years an increase of piety, devotion, Sabbath observance, and the like, and that we might rather have looked for those blessings which are promised in the Scriptures, that we should " ride on the high places of the earth," and " be like a watered garden." (*Isaiah* lviii. 14.) I cannot bring myself to believe that the present war is a divine judgment inflicted on us for pre-eminence in Sabbath breaking, profanity, incontinence, cupidity, or luxury. Will any one say that our peculiar national distinction is any one or all of these vices? Even the love of money is no more peculiar to us than to the English, the Scotch, or the Germans.

The real and only cause of the present troubles is Slavery, nothing else. Had there been no slavery, there would have been no war. This is the truth. It cannot be disguised. There is nothing gained by trying to ignore it. There is no use in handling it delicately, and speaking of it *sotto voce*. The time for being mealy-mouthed, if it ever was, is over. The stern arbitrament of war has been resorted to, and we may as well know distinctly what it is we are spending so much blood and treasure for.

The South does not hesitate to say openly and unequivocally that she is fighting for the perpetuation and extension of slavery. The Confederacy, says Vice-President Stephens, " is founded on the idea, its corner-stone rests upon it." General Polk, the modern Leonidas who has devoted himself with Spartan self-abnegation to the cause, and who, being a Right Reverend as well as a Brigadier-General, may be regarded both as a soldier and a saint, affirms that he is contending " for principles which lie at the foundation of their social, political and religious polity, and that they are the best bulwark of civilization." Dr. Palmer of New Orleans, chimes in with these views, declaring it to be the " mission of the South to conserve and perpetuate" to future generations, the peculiar institution. Why, then, should any one in these high latitudes, be sensitive about alluding to this subject. Why not come right out, like John Knox, and call a fig, a fig, a spade, a spade.

Nor is anything more susceptible of proof than that the North did not begin this war. So far from it, the North seemed to be stupefied and paralyzed, and unwilling to credit the ruin that was spreading under its eyes. It looked on with astounding apathy, and saw fort after fort, arsenal after arsenal, custom-house after custom-house, navy-yard after navy-yard, ship after ship, stolen more or less openly, battery after battery erected, State after State seceded, till it became a butt for ridicule on account of its forbearance and pusillanimity. Plainly the curse denounced on those blood-thirsty wretches who are the first to take the sword, and who shall therefore fall by the sword, cannot be, with any appearance of likelihood, impending over the North.

It is charged that a deep-laid scheme was laid years ago, some say as long ago as thirty years, and that the plot has been systematically and persistently kept up, to prepare the heart of the Southern people for this issue; while Southern men, high in office, were clandestinely transferring munitions of war, scattering the navy, and crippling the Treasury, for the benefit of the South and the weakening of the North. The history of the Republic confirms the statement; and it is only necessary, in order to trace the plan in its cunning and wide-spread ramifications, to advert to Cuba, Texas, the Mexican war, the repeal of the Missouri compromise, Kansas and Lecompton; or to refer to McDuffie's speeches, Calhoun's writings, and the Partisan Leader.

Any one that was on the stage of active life thirty years ago, knows that there was then a tolerable degree of unanimity on the slavery question. Slavery was acknowledged to be an evil, and was excused and apologized for. Abolitionism had not yet shown its teeth. Garrison was yet below the horizon. The Colonization Society was regarded as the great safety-valve, under the blessing of Providence. One of the largest colonization meetings ever held, was held about that date, in the city of Lexington, Kentucky, in the capacious Methodist Church, at which Mr. Clay and Robert Wickliffe, Senior, the two great men of the vicinity, made speeches. In Mr. Clay's speech occurred the following memorable sentiment, which I give in his very words, uttered, and uttered without rebuke, in the ears of all Lexington, "SLAVERY IS A CURSE TO THE MASTER, AND A WRONG, A GRIEVOUS WRONG, TO THE SLAVE." In those days such men as Judge Green, Judge Underwood, Rev. Robert J. Breckenridge, President Young, and others of the wise and good of Kentucky, stood and labored in the same cause, shoulder to shoulder.

The South has shifted its ground since that time. Mr. Stephens, to whose words the office of Vice-President may lend greater weight, expressly declares there has been a change, and takes credit for having left the old fogy notions of our Revolutionary sires, and for having laid an entirely novel and before unthought of basis for the truest civilization. He tells us, that "the general opinion of the men of that day was, that somehow or other, in the order of Providence, the institution would be evanescent and pass away. This idea, though not incorporated in the Constitution, was the prevailing idea at that time. * * * *
These ideas, however, were fundamentally wrong. They rested upon the assumption of an equality of races. This was an error. Our new government is founded upon entirely the contrary idea. * * * *
Its foundations are laid, its corner-stone rests upon the great truth that the negro is not equal to the white man, that slavery, subordination to the superior race, is his natural and normal condition. This truth has been slow in the process of its development, like all other truths in the various departments of science. It has been so among us. Many who hear me, perhaps, can recollect well that this truth was not generally admitted, even within their day. The errors of the

past generation still clung to many as late as twenty years ago."

It is not necessary to cite other testimony after so bold and unequivocal a statement as this. If further evidence is demanded, we may refer to Mr. Everett's Fourth of July speech, which effectually disposes of other issues as trivial. It must be admitted that while the North has not changed, while the Constitution remains unaltered, while the Government has bent all its efforts to keep the Constitution inviolate, while the new President in advance pledged his determination to trespass on no vested rights, and while Congress, with unparalleled unanimity, has recently disavowed any project of conquest or subjugation, or any other purpose than simply to maintain the supremacy of the laws and the integrity of the Union, the South has drifted from its old moorings, and is at sea under a press of canvass destined for an entirely different harbor. Indeed the South did not wait for any actual inroad, but with indecent haste proclaimed secession before the new President was inaugurated, and having but its fears and anticipations to justify the course. So long as it could have its own way, and dominate over a subservient North, and dictate the laws, and occupy the territories, and direct all measures for the strengthening of its own peculiar interests, the South had no objection to stay in the Union; but the moment a President came into office, no matter how lawfully, whose opinions and administration were looked on with suspicion, every tie must be severed, and the Union, like the old Confederation which it superseded, proclaimed no better than a rope of sand.

Since then, all other issues are irrelevant, and slavery is, and by the South is openly avowed to be, the sole occasion of the present agitations, we may approach the consideration of another point, viz.: How far is the North culpable, and is the present war to be viewed in the light of a special judgment upon the North?

If the North has not changed its ground, and if it has not been growing morally worse of late years, then it is difficult to see how the North has made itself obnoxious to any special judgment of this nature. On the contrary, the North appears to have waked up at last to take a step in the right direction. Finding that yielding had gone as far as it could without sacrificing every vestige of manly independence, the North has determined to make no further concessions, and to shake off all responsibility for extending or perpetuating the area of slavery. As a local institution, slavery can have no vitality nor rights outside of the locality in which it obtains. Slavery, says the South, is national, Freedom is sectional. No! cries the North, in a voice of thunder, Slavery is sectional, Freedom is national!

Now I beg leave to ask, when the North is taking a stand for the Constitution, for the traditions of the Fathers, for the dictates of Natural Law, and for the cause of Humanity, are we to be told, this is the moment which Divine Providence has selected of all others, to array its vengeance against us, and hurl its judgments on our heads! Why, if there be a guilty party, against whom those judgments would seem more worthily due, should it not rather be the South, which has removed the ancient landmarks, proclaimed war for the maintenance and extension of slavery, and struck the first blow in an unnatural, horrid and fratricidal contest? To the South war may be, and doubtless will prove, a severe and tremendous judgment. To the North it may wear another aspect.

The dealings of Providence, even the troubles and afflictions which He permits to befal us, are not always punitive. They are sometimes only disciplinary. They are not judgments, but trials. They are intended to separate the gold from the dross, the wheat from the chaff, and to develope something refined and valuable. No one is entitled, therefore, from the mere existence of agitation or trouble, to infer some great preceding crime as the cause. This was the mistake Job's well-meaning but narrow-minded friends fell into. It was the error of those who thought the Galileans who were crushed beneath the tower of Siloam must be sinners above all the Galileans. It was the prejudice which the disciples fostered, when they asked concerning the blind man, which had sinned, he or his parents, that he had been born blind? Every affliction is not necessarily a judgment; it may be sent as a great means of moral discipline.

But still further, we do not see the evidences that this war is a judgment. It is readily conceded that War, Pestilence and Famine, are severe evils, and to be deprecated. Of these, it is also admitted, that David chose pestilence rather than war; but it was war in the form of defeat, fleeing three months before pursuing and relentless enemies, not war in its victorious phase. There has been great interruption of commerce, a stagnation of business, an extensive bankruptcy, and much suffering. But much of this distress may be directly traced to the non-payment of the enormous debts due from the South, which the South declines paying in the present position of affairs. The commercial prostration is believed to be temporary. Business is reviving, and recovering on a more solid basis of cash rather than credit. Western harvests are prolific. Our exports exceed our imports. We are contracting no outstanding foreign debt. Specie is flowing in upon us, instead of being drained out. Factories are re-opened. The Government has had no difficulty in raising the vast sum of $500,000,000. This amount, in addition to $200,000,000, already disbursed, has been, or will be obtained within our own borders. We have not had to go out of the country to borrow a dollar. The Rothschilds may keep kings, kaisers and popes in leading strings, and under obligations to them, but they have no hold on the United States. The people, with a generous confidence in the stability and resources of the Republic, press forward with their offerings to lend to the Government. All this vast amount of money, as it is raised, is to be expended amongst ourselves. Somebody gets it. It is not lost. It is not thrown into the sea. It is not sent away. It circulates among the community. Trade, for a moment impeded, follows the laws of trade, and seeks out new channels. Capital will once more be active. The laboring classes will again find employment. Prosperity will revisit the land. The people will be no worse off for curtailing some of their business, and practicing that rare virtue, economy.

Meantime, we have fouud out, and the world has found out, *that we have a Government.* At one time, that point seemed problematical. It is now satisfactorily settled. We have a government. Add to this, that a check has been put to growing political and civic corruption, which was fast bringing popular institutions into disrepute. The uprising of a great people at the sound of the first gun against Fort Sumter, has attracted the admiration of mankind, and is one of those instances of the morally sublime, which will shine with peculiar lustre on the pages of future history. It has redeemed this generation from the charge of indifference to everything but money-making. Party lines have been obliterated, and men of all shades of opinion unite for their country. Our young men lately in danger of being spoiled and enervated by prosperity, now see a noble and animating career opening before them. Sublime sentiments fire their hearts. They spring to arms. They submit to self-denial. They inure themselves to hardships. They bare their bosoms to peril. They devote their lives, with prodigal unselfishness, to the service of their country. They are saved from luxury, idleness, and an aimless life. They are developing themselves into heroes. Their families and their country are proud of them.

Thus then, war, with all its concomitant annoyances, is not the worst of evils. It is not an unmitigated evil. It has its palliations. It has its dark side, but it also has its columnar glory. The Tribes on their way out of the wilderness into the Promised Land, were under the necessity of fighting with nation after nation, and king after king, that rose up to dispute their progress.

But I have never heard that military necessity represented as a judgment upon those heaven-directed tribes. It was a judgment on the crushed and defeated Canaanites, but it served to give energy, confidence, and character to the Hebrews, and that whole generation who were contemporary with Joshua remained steadfast to the principles of religion and truth.

> "Knowledge, by suffering entereth,
> And Life is perfected by Death."

The historian Alison has some sentiments strikingly coincident with the opinions just expressed, which are worth quoting.

"It is in periods of apparent disaster, during the suffering of whole generations, that the greatest improvements on human character have been effected, and a foundation laid for those changes which ultimately prove most beneficial to the species. The wars of the Heptarchy, the Norman Conquest, the Contest of the Roses, the Great Rebellion, are apparently the most disastrous periods of our annals; those in which civil discord was most furious, and the public suffering most universal. Yet these are precisely the periods in which its peculiar temper was given to the English character, and the greatest addition made to the causes of English prosperity; in which courage arose out of the extremity of misfortune, national union out of oppression, public emancipation out of aristocratic dissension, general freedom out of regal ambition. The national character which we now possess, the public benefits we now enjoy, the freedom by which we have been distinguished, the energy by which we are sustained, are in a great measure owing to the renovating storms, which have, in former ages, passed over our country."—*Hist. Eur. Vol. I., c. 1.*

It was by hardihood and patience the Dutch Republic gained the recognition of its rights. It was by a succession of wars, sometimes foreign, sometimes civil, that England secured her constitutional liberties. It was not till after an arduous struggle of eight years that the United States achieved their independence, and entered upon their career of greatness as a power on the earth. This war, then, may be regarded not as a judgment, indicative of the divine displeasure, but as a season of trial and discipline, out of which the total nationality shall emerge ere long, and rise to a loftier plane than it has yet reached. We have passed successfully through several wars, each of which has left us gainers. The first gave us independence. The second secured us the command of the sea, and the respect of the world. The third put in our hands the entire continent stretching to the Pacific. We are now to show whether we can stand the test of Civil War, and vindicate the National Unity, and the supremacy of the Constitution. If we come triumphantly out of this test, the Republic may be considered as having a brighter future before her than ever.

Thus far my task has been one of discrimination. As a public teacher of morals, I am as much bound by conscience as any one else, to tell what I believe to be the truth, not what other persons believe to be the truth; to distinguish carefully the truth from error, and to separate the wheat from the chaff. I must "deliver my soul." I have endeavored to set aside all erroneous issues and put the subject in a full and clear light. We often approximate to the truth by first eliminating every element of error.

I will now proceed to show some of the true grounds we have for humiliation, and to point out the national sins of which we should repent. We have as a people, as a nation, as a Church, as individuals, reason enough to bow low before the Searcher of hearts, and implore forgiveness.

We should feel humbled to think of the *occasion* of this war, we who have been proud of our high civilization,

" We, the heirs of all the ages, foremost in the files of time."

Slavery has been long felt and lamented as the one plague-spot of the Republic, the great blot on our escutcheon. It is this that has exposed as to the taunts of Europe, and cut off our churches from ecclesiastical fellowship with the great historical churches of the Old World. It is in vain for the North to repudiate all complicity. The national solidarity exposes all parts to reproach for the faults of any single one. When a calamity befals a particular denomination of Christians, the others have no right to exult, for the world confounds all together, and points at all alike, as joint professors of the same religion; just so, we must accept the inconveniences of that national unity to maintain which in its integrity we are now in arms. With it we must consent to share the perils or the reproaches of each particular section. It is a scandal that may make us all blush, that it was in the bosom of the United States were reared so many traitors, perjurers, and robbers. The whole Republic stands disgraced because such men as Cobb, and Floyd, and Twiggs, were her children. They, like ourselves, are Americans. As Americans, as citizens of the United States, we have cause to hang our heads, to think that Benedict Arnold was not the last of his race.

If we honestly think Slavery to be at the bottom of all this trouble, and accountable for the war and all its horrors, and if this consideration makes us less in love with the system than ever, we do right in humbly but earnestly praying that the nuisance may be abated, and the impediment to national unity and prosperity be removed. While our hands are tied by constitutional compacts, so that we have no right to interfere with the local institutions of the South, we can, at least, pray that Divine Providence in its wisdom, may overrule the present agitation in some way, that human wisdom does not clearly see, to bring about some modification or amelioration of the system, leading to its ultimate, but safe, gradual, and peaceful, extinction.

Providence appears to be acting on a uniform plan all over the rest of the world, " to break every yoke and let the oppressed go free," why should we suppose America the sole exception, the sole lazar-house, left in the civilized world, where the fetter is to be more strongly riveted, and emancipation rendered forever hopeless. What changes war may yet bring about, as it has already brought about some, or to what measures urgent military necessities may compel, or what new cotton fields may be thrown open to the world, is not patent to the eye at present, but we can hardly doubt that the future is pregnant with great improvements and possible benedictions. At all events, we can pray.

I see great cause for humiliation on account of *the check given to our arms*. Though the war has been planned on a gigantic scale, and though months have passed, our armies are still on the defensive. We have sustained repeated checks and reverses, from the capture of Sumpter to the surrender of Lexington. The panic at Bull Run was a most humiliating affair. And let it be remembered that panics are denounced by Jehovah as one of his instruments of displeasure. If a people provoke Him " they shall flee seven ways before their enemies. How should one chase a thousand, and two put ten thousand to flight, except their Rock had sold them, and the Lord had shut them up?" And what do we see now ? Missouri overrun, Kentucky invaded, privateers active, the national capital beleaguered, and the insurgent flag flaunting defiance in sight of the Federal city, and there is no Ellsworth to pluck it down! Neither do we know what is to be the result of this conflict. Since the numerous reverses and even disgraceful retreats that have occurred, we have no title to expect uninterrupted success. Our troops have not shown themselves invincible. Collisions may occur with foreign nations. England withholds her sympathy. We can hardly indeed expect proud aristocracies and venerable monarchies to evince a cordial love for Republican institutions. They scarcely repress their exultation. " Aha! aha!" they say, " so would we have it. This is the day that we looked for, we have found, we have seen it. We told you so, you discontented Plebeians. It is as we predicted. The model republic is dead. The bubble has burst!"

It may be further remarked, that if we have one national sin that distinguishes us more than another, it is the passion of *covetousness*. Our greed has been the world's proverb. Not that we are worse than some other nations, or are miserly, or are given to hoarding, or to love money for its own sake. But the rage for display, the love of luxury, the outvieing every body else, the lust of ostentation, the longing to have wherewithal to spend, the haste to be rich, these are prevalent motives, and they require fuel to minister to their gratification. Slaveholding in the South, and the fitting out of scores of slavers in Northern cities, are both but exemplications of the same engrossing passion for wealth and greed of gain. For such a propensity we may well be ashamed and repent in dust and ashes, as a nation and as individuals. This is the parent of all the venality and corruption, of the repeated embezzlement and defalcations, of the frauds in army and navy contracts, that have stained our annals from one end of the country to the other.

Further, *we have been too prone to self-glorification.* We are noted for our national vanity. Bragging is an infirmity of the entire people. Providence has evidently designed to curb us, and to abate our overweening self-confidence. God seems to say to us as he did once to the Jews, " I will curse your blessings." We have made our parchment Constitution our idol. Under its ægis nothing could harm us. " Come, all ye nations of the world, imitate our example, and take shelter beneath the shadow of our wings!" We have to some extent profited by the wholesome rebukes we have sustained. The tone of the public press, and the tone of our orators, is not so arrogant as it was. We have learned that the struggle is to be a desperate one, and we must not undervalue our antagonists. We have been taught the value of military discipline and respect for authority. We have found that an undisciplined mob in uniform is not an army. We have learned that military science does not come by nature, nor is absorbed through the donning of a pair of epaulets. We have learned the need of caution, and good generalship, that the lives of our really brave and noble troops may not be thrown away for lack of a head to direct them. Well will it be for us then, if among the lessons of the hour we learn humility, as well as humiliation.

Much more might be said, but I shall only add, that if we would succeed we must repent of our tendency to rely on "the arm of flesh," and *trust in Providence.* We must reverence God's holy Sabbath, we must respect the Holy Name, we must banish irregularity and vice from the camp, and every where else. Because a man is a soldier, it is thought he is dispensed from the Moral Law. "There is no Sabbath," we are told, "in war." And so, movements have been made, regiments transported, colors given, reviews ordered, battles fought, on the Sabbath. The Chaplain of the House of Representatives, Mr. Stockton, has stated that the battle of Bull Run was arranged on the Sabbath day to suit the convenience of certain Congressmen and civilians, who wanted to see it as a gladiatorial combat, (and some of them have seen more than they wanted.) Many pious people have believed that God permitted a shameful and totally unnecessary panic to sully our arms, (up to that point victorious,) in order to vindicate his holy day, and testify his displeasure at its unnecessary violation. They see the attestation of this in the disastrous termination of every battle, without exception, offered on the Sabbath day; Plattsburg, New Orleans, Waterloo, and Bull Run. Let us accept it as a token for good that the gallant commander on the Potomac has issued a general order for the better observance of the Sabbath, and that no unnecessary drills, parades, reviews, or engagements are to be permitted by him henceforth.

We cannot, Oh, ye politicians! we cannot, oh, ye worldly-wise Statesmen! afford to dispense with the aid of God. Napoleon I. said, (although some doubt whether he said it,) "Providence favors the strong battalions." In the rout and disappearance of the Xerxes-like host which he precipitated upon Russia, the impious sneer was disproved. The ultimate success of the Prince of Orange against the haughty chivalry of Spain, disproves it. The repulse of the Armada disproves it. The existence of this republic disproves it. The emancipation of Italy disproves it. The retiring of the Assyrian king from before the walls of Jerusalem disproves it. The history of Gideon and the Midianites disproves it.

Let us not " sacrifice to our net, or burn incense to our drag;" let us not " take the corn, and wine, and oil, the silver and the gold, which Jehovah has given us, and prepare it for Baal." Let us honor the Lord that made us, that preserves us, and that redeems us. Let us faithfully reverence his name and observe his institutions. Let us put our trust in God, and constantly invoke his protection. Let our petition be to the throne of grace, "Give us help from trouble! for vain is the help of man." Then " through God we shall do valiantly: for he it is that shall tread down our enemies."